GREEK THEATRE

Stewart Ross

PETER BEDRICK BOOKS
INCORPORATED

ANCIENT GREECE
Daily Life
Gods and Goddesses
Greek Theatre
The Original Olympics

Front cover: A marble sculpture showing both
tragic and comic ancient Greek theatre masks.

Series editors: Katrina Maitland Smith and Jill A. Laidlaw
Book editor: Jill A. Laidlaw
Design: Stonecastle Graphics Ltd
Consultant: Dr. Angus M. Bowie, Lobel Fellow in Classics at
the Queen's College, University of Oxford

Published in the United States in 1999
by Peter Bedrick Books
A division of NTC/Contemporary Publishing Group, Inc.
4255 West Touhy Avenue, Lincolnwood (Chicago), Illinois 60646-1975 U.S.A.

Ross, Stewart.
    Greek Theatre/Stewart Ross.
        p.   cm. -- (Ancient Greece)
    Includes bibliographical references (p.47) and index.
    Summary: A history of ancient Greel drama including discussion of the drama
competition, Oedipus the King, actors and the chorus, playwrights, and the legacy of
Greece.
        ISBN 0-87226-597-8
        1. Greek Drama--History and criticis--Juvenile literature.
    2. Theater--Greece--History--Juvenile literature.   [1. Greek drama--History and
Criticism.   2. Theater--Greece--History.]   I. Title.
II. Series: Ancient Greece (Peter Bedrick Books)
PA3131.R65   1999
882.0109--DC20   95-25017
                                                                         CIP

Typesetting and reproduction by Pageturn Ltd.
Printed and bound by Eurografica, Italy

International Standard Book Number: 0-87226-597-8
99 00 01 02 03 10 9 8 7 6 5 4 3 2 1

CONTENTS

A bronze statue of a comic
actor wearing a mask,
from the fourth century BC.

1 The Drama Competition

It is an hour before sunrise on a fine spring morning in the city of Athens, about 2,500 years ago. Woken by their slaves, three actors wash and eat a hasty breakfast before hurrying down to the theatre. There they greet the men of the chorus and prepare for their performance.

The play is *Oedipus the King*, written by the great poet Sophocles. The actors are nervous, particularly the protagonist. The protagonist is the main actor, who will play the part of King Oedipus. *Oedipus the King* is one of a group of plays chosen to enter Athens' annual drama competition. If the play wins, the poet, actors and producer will receive prizes and great honor.

The Greek god Dionysus, at whose festival plays were performed. This is a scene from a legend that said that vine leaves grew from the mast of a ship Dionysus was sailing.

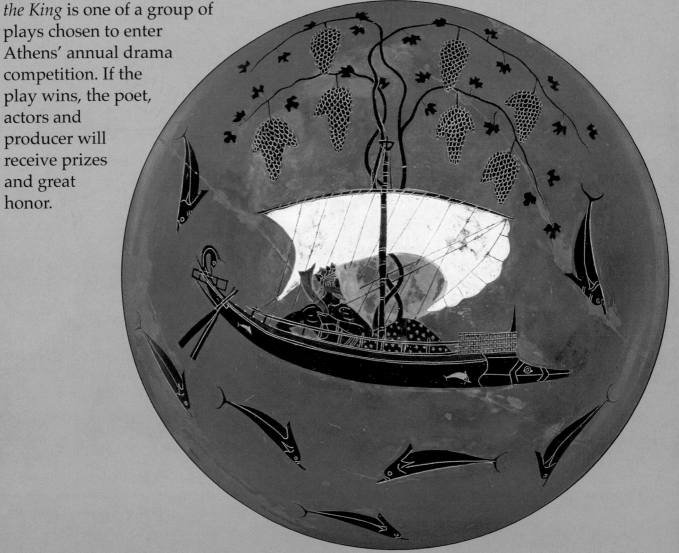

Dionysus

The drama competition is part of one of Athens' most popular religious festivals, known as the City Dionysia. It is held every year in honor of the god Dionysus, also known as Bacchus.

Dionysus is the Greek god of wine, new life and illusion (things not being what they appear to be). Dionysus rules the world of passion and horror, not reason. The Greeks believe that he sometimes takes the shape of a goat or a bull. Frightening Greek legends tell of people and gods who anger Dionysus being torn to pieces by his excited women followers, called *maenads*.

Dionysus is also a god of fertility. He makes sure that people have children. The Greeks believe the world will die without Dionysus. Because of this, Dionysus holds a special place in the hearts of all Greeks. Not surprisingly, most towns and villages around Athens – known as *demes* – have their own Dionysian festivals, called the Rural Dionysia.

A maenad with a leopard and an ivy-wreathed staff, both of which were associated with Dionysus.

" . . . Athens, that holy land of freedom
Where famous wisdom lives . . . "

Euripides, *Medea*, 431 BC.

ΚΛΜΝΞΟΠΡΣΤΥΦΧΨΩ

Φ
Χ
Ψ

The City Dionysia is attended by Athenians and visitors from all over the Greek-speaking world. Drama is a key part of the festival. The theatre in Athens is attached to the temple of Dionysus, where a statue of the god stands. The festival begins with a ceremony that reminds Athenians that Dionysus came to Athens from the town of Eleutherae. The statue of the god is carried from the temple to the outskirts of Eleutherae, then brought back to Athens by the light of flaming torches.

Other celebrations follow over the next few days. These include a lively procession through the crowded streets and a ceremony in which tribute money from Athens' allies is handed over.

Now that the celebrations are over, the main part of the festival – the presentation of new plays – is underway.

At the theatre

Shortly after dawn the audience begins to arrive. The actors run quickly through their lines, muttering to themselves in the shadows. As there is no prompter, they have to remember all their words perfectly.

The god Dionysus appeared as a character in many plays. In *Frogs* by Aristophanes (405 BC), Dionysus says how much he misses the playwright Euripides!

"I am desperate to see poor old Euripides again, him that's dead and gone."

Λ Μ Ν Ξ Ο Π Ρ Σ Τ Υ Φ Χ Ψ
Υ Φ Χ Ψ Ω

A figure carved out of stone from the theatre of Dionysus in Athens.

Sophocles arrives, has a chat with the protagonist and wishes all the actors luck. They are also visited by the *choregos*, the wealthy citizen who is paying for the chorus and other parts of the production. The choregos stands to gain as much honor and fame as the poet if the play that he has funded wins.

Before long, the enormous theatre is filled to bursting. The judges take their places in the front row. Trumpets blare. Oedipus, king of Thebes, enters.

Amid a babble of expectation, the play begins.

A Roman fresco wall painting showing a scene from a ceremony associated with Dionysus. The Romans also worshiped Dionysus. The mask is from Greek theatre.

2 *Oedipus the King*

In the play *Oedipus the King*, Oedipus is a strong and wise king. He left Corinth, where he believed he was born, because an oracle told him that he would kill his father, the king of Corinth, and marry his mother.

A stone carving of Oedipus meeting the Sphinx.

A marble sculpture of Sophocles. This is a Roman copy of a Greek original made in the fourth century BC, so it may be quite a good likeness of the great playwright.

King of Thebes

Oedipus traveled to the city of Thebes, whose king (called Laius) had been killed. The people of Thebes made Oedipus their king because he had saved them from a monster called the Sphinx. Oedipus correctly answered a riddle the Sphinx had asked: "What thing goes on four legs in the morning, two legs in the middle of the day and three legs in the evening?" The answer is a man who crawls as a child, walks on two legs when grown up, but needs a stick when he grows old. Oedipus gets married to Iocasta, the widow of the previous king of Thebes.

Plague

A dreadful plague rages through the city of Thebes, and the people ask Oedipus to save them.

"Today, O great and mighty Oedipus!
On bended knee all citizens beg you
To come to their rescue . . . "

Oedipus says that he has already sent his brother-in-law, Creon, to ask the oracle how to get rid of the plague. Creon returns and says that the plague will go when they drive out or kill the man who slew Laius, the last king of Thebes. Oedipus promises to find this person.

He seeks the advice of an old blind seer called Teiresias. Oedipus is furious at what Teiresias says:

"The killer whom you seek is here –
yourself!"

Teiresias tells Oedipus that, although he has eyes, he is blind to the truth. He warns Oedipus:

"Today you'll meet with both your
birth and fall!"

A sinister feeling has come over

The terrible prophecy

Oedipus thinks that Teiresias is plotting with Creon to get rid of him. Oedipus and Creon have a furious argument. Hearing the noise, Oedipus' wife Iocasta comes in and they explain what is going on.

There is no need to worry, Iocasta says. King Laius, her first husband, had once been told that he would be killed by his own son at a place where three roads meet. In fact, he was killed by robbers, and her son by King Laius was left to die on a mountain track while still a baby. So there is no way Oedipus could have killed Laius. But the king is not consoled:

"One thing you have told me, Iocasta,
Fills me with terror to my very soul."

Once Oedipus killed a man where three roads meet. The prophecy of his youth, that he would kill his father and marry his mother, looks as if it might be true!

A vase painting from the fifth century BC showing a scene from *Oedipus the King*.

A Roman mosaic (a picture made of small colored stones or glass) of a female mask used in Greek tragedy. The mouths on masks were always open, so that the actors' voices could be heard.

The fall of Oedipus

Two shepherds, one from Thebes and one from Corinth, rescued Iocasta's baby son. The baby was Oedipus. It was he, not robbers, who killed King Laius. After becoming king of Thebes, Oedipus married Laius' widow – his own mother!

The truth fills Iocasta and Oedipus with horror and shame. Iocasta hangs herself. Believing death is too good for him, Oedipus digs out his eyes with the pins of Iocasta's brooches.

"As quickly as you can," he begs the chorus,

"Send me to another land or kill me!
Let the deepest sea cover me over.
Do not touch anyone as cursed as me!
You have nothing to fear, for I alone
Must carry the weight of my dreadful sin."

The play ends as Oedipus is led away, blind and broken.

3 The Worship of Dionysus

Greek drama began long before Sophocles and his play about King Oedipus (which is from the fifth century BC). Scholars think that Greek drama grew out of special ceremonies, particularly religious ones. In ceremonies worshiping the god Dionysus, groups of men danced and sang together. To begin with, they made up the words and movements as they went along. The song and dance were called a *dithyramb*.

In time, the dithyramb became more organized. Those taking part were arranged as a chorus. Their words and movements were written down and learned by heart. Chanting and singing were used to tell stories as well as to praise Dionysus.

Homer

The greatest poet of the early Greek world was Homer. Almost nothing is known about this remarkable man, who lived in the eighth century BC. He is supposed to have been the author of two magnificent epic poems, the *Iliad* and the *Odyssey*. These poems influenced Greek writing for many years to come.

The poets who wrote the dithyramb choruses knew Homer's work. They liked the way he compared the weakness of men with the power of the gods. They admired his heroes and heroines and the beautiful way he used language.

An imaginary portrait of Homer. This sculpture, made in the second century AD, is a copy of one made four centuries earlier.

Actors holding their masks make offerings to Dionysus. One of the god's followers is seated on the couch with him.

Homer's work is filled with feelings of pity for the human race:

"Of all the creatures, Man is most forlorn
That in the ocean or on land are born."

The *Iliad*, eighth century BC.

ZHΘIKAMNΞ

ΦΧΨΩ

Dithyramb stories

At first, a dithyramb was not a play. It was a song-and-dance performance by a chorus of about fifty men. The performers did not pretend to be anyone else — they did not act. But then, in the seventh century BC, men such as Arion began using the dithyramb to tell stories.

The important change came when one person began to speak separately from the chorus. Greek tradition says that the poet Thespis was the first person to do this. In other words, he became an actor.

A fifth century BC vase painting showing a chorus of young warriors singing.

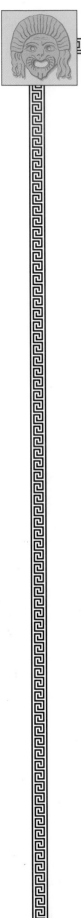

Chorus and actors

To begin with, plays were performed by a chorus and one actor. In time, a second actor was used, then a third. A chorus and three actors became the tradition. Until the time of Sophocles, the poet himself was one of the main actors.

When the actors appeared, the chorus remained half in the action and half out of it. The chorus in *Oedipus the King* represents the elders of Thebes. They talk to the actors and are an important part of the play. But they also comment on the story as if they are in the audience.

The ruins of the theatre of Dionysus at Athens. The orchestra (see also page 31) can still be clearly seen, but little remains behind it.

Tragedy

The Greeks called the later dithyrambs and the first plays "tragedies," from the word *tragoidia*, meaning "goat song." This expression probably comes from the custom of sacrificing a goat to Dionysus or giving a goat as a prize for the best drama. The name "tragedy" remained when the prizes were no longer goats. It came to mean a serious and often sad play.

> *"Tragedy does not show men, but life and action."*
>
> Aristotle, *Poetics*, fourth century BC.

Φ
Χ
Ψ
ΝΞΟΠΡΣΤΥΦΧΨΩ

Satyr plays

Satyr plays were dramas about legendary creatures who were half human and half goat. These animals were followers of Dionysus. Satyr plays became part of the City Dionysia in 501 BC.

Comedies

Comedies, like tragedies, were connected to the worship of Dionysus. In the sixth century BC, following the example of more serious dramas, comedies began to be performed in one place, year after year. For some time they were put on by volunteers.

In 486 BC, however, they became a formal part of the City Dionysia.

Stone statues of actors in comic masks. They represent (from left to right) an elderly slave, a man from the country, and a "parasite," someone who goes from table to table exchanging entertaining conversations for food.

4 The Minor Festivals

The greatest Greek drama was written and performed in Athens and its surrounding towns and villages. This area is known as Attica. When we speak of ancient Greek drama, we usually mean the drama of Attica.

Plays were only performed as part of religious festivals. Unlike today, plays were usually given only one performance at each festival. No theatre remained open the year round.

The festivals

Festivals were very important to the people of Attica. They were more than religious occasions. These were times for

This map shows the boundaries of the ancient Greek-speaking world and Attica, the center of Greek drama.

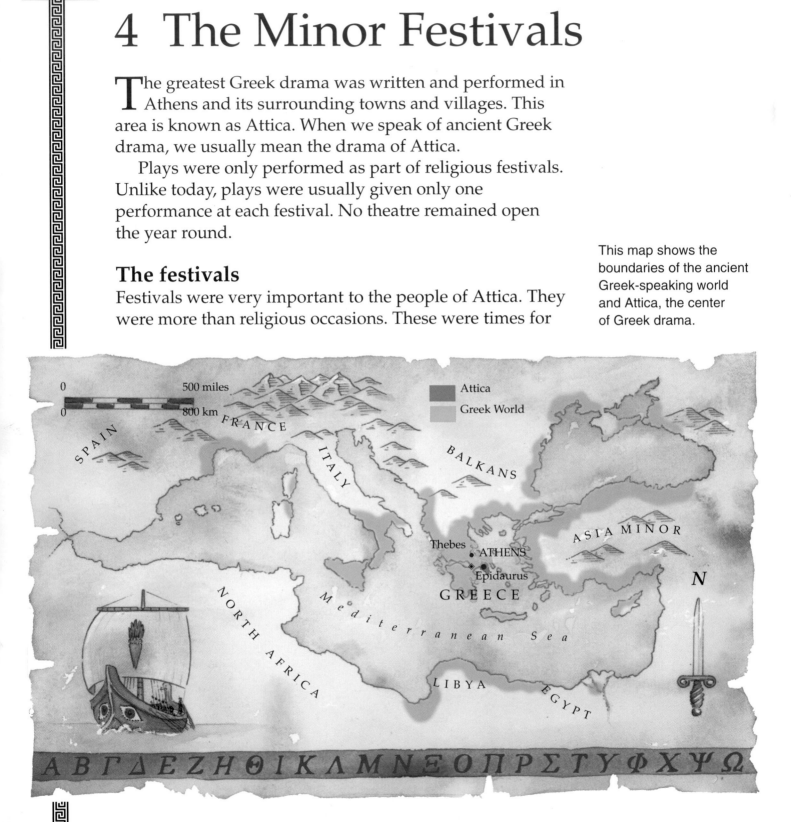

The Lenaea

The annual Lenaea festival was held in Athens at the end of January. The details of what went on are not at all clear. We think that it began in the Lenaeum, an area set aside for the worship of Dionysus, but we do not know where this was. Some time after the middle of the fifth century BC, the Lenaea plays were performed in the main theatre in Athens.

The festival included a procession and, after about 440 BC, a drama competition. Unlike the City Dionysia, at which *Oedipus the King* was probably first performed, the Lenaea's plays were mostly comedies. Five comic playwrights and two tragic playwrights took part. The competition attracted the best comedy writers but few really good tragedy writers.

The Acropolis, in Athens, as it is today.

"We know the world is a wonderful place, And finest of all is the human race."

Sophocles, *Antigone*, fifth century BC.

ΚΛΜΝΞΟΠΡΣΤΥΦΧΨΩ

Φ
Χ
Ψ

A vase that shows
the gods fighting
(top) and people in a
Dionysiac procession
(bottom). This vase
dates from 460 BC.

The Anthesteria

Most of the gods were honored in festivals all over Greece. The Anthesteria was a Dionysian festival at which drama was performed. It took place in Spring, probably February or March, and it had elements of celebration and rejoicing, and of gloom and mourning.

Scholars believe that on the first day of the Anthesteria, jars of the previous year's wine were opened and some of the contents drunk. The second day was devoted to a drinking contest. It ended with a secret ceremony. This was a pretend marriage between Dionysus and the wife of the Chief Archon, one of Athens' city officials. The third day was much more serious. It was set aside for remembering the dead, particularly those of one's own family.

At some time during the festival, a huge procession wound through the streets with an image of Dionysus carried in a cart. We are not sure exactly what drama was performed at the Anthesteria. All we know is that there was dancing and contests between actors.

The god Dionysus riding in a cart with Ariadne, his wife. She was the daughter of King Minos of Crete. The cart is pulled by pipe-playing centaurs, mythical creatures that were half-man, half-horse.

Rural Dionysia

These local festivals were put on in the late winter or early spring, but not all at the same time. There were processions with symbols of fertility, sacrifices, drinking, games, singing and dancing.

By the fifth century BC, quite a few Rural Dionysia included dithyramb, comedy or tragedy, or a combination of all three. Some people enjoyed the plays so much that they travelled around from one Rural Dionysia to another following the productions. Larger demes had their own theatres. The ruins of some of these can be seen today.

5 The City Dionysia

By far the most important Dionysian festival was the one at which *Oedipus the King* was performed, the City Dionysia. It was sometimes known as the Great Dionysia, or simply the Dionysia.

The City Dionysia was staged at the end of March. At this time of year, traveling was easier, and people came to the festival from all over the Greek-speaking world. We have evidence of what went on from several sources, the plays themselves, the writings of other ancient Greeks, archeology and paintings on vases. Scholars have pieced together this evidence to produce a fairly clear picture of what the City Dionysia was like when Greek drama was at its best, in the fifth century BC.

The archon

The City Dionysia was run by one of nine magistrates chosen from among the citizens every year. This magistrate was known as the *archon*. The archon served for a year and was paid for his work. He had two assistants. Organizing the festival was only one of his many jobs for the city.

The archon may have begun work on the festival ten months before it took place. Because it was a religious occasion, priests helped him to organize the rituals.

These people are drinking a toast to Dionysus. The clothes they are wearing would have been worn by citizens of Athens.

Choosing the poets

One of the archon's first tasks was to choose the poets whose plays were to be performed. Tragedy writers had to offer three tragedies and a satyr play. Comedy writers put forward just one play each.

It is not clear how the archon made his choice. He may have selected the most famous playwrights, or he may have asked the poets to read some of their work to him. Only three tragedy writers were given the honor of having their work performed. It is worth remembering that the poets were not just interested in performance. The festival drama was a competition – they wanted to win!

This is part of a mosaic, made in Cyprus in the third century AD, showing King Icarius being taught wine-making by Dionysus. Cyprus was part of the ancient Greek-speaking world.

ΙΚΑΡΙΟC

"*At Thebes I have arrived today,*
Zeus' great son Dionysus."

Euripides, *Bacchae*, c. 406 BC.

Φ
Χ
Ψ

ΚΛΜΝΞΟΠΡΣΤΥΦΧΨΩ

The choregoi

Like today, putting on a play in ancient Greece was an expensive business. To help with the costs, the archon selected a number of wealthy citizens who were called choregoi. Each choregos was allocated to a poet by lot. It was the choregos' task to find and pay for a chorus of fifteen men and musicians for four plays. The choregos also had to pay for masks, costumes, props (objects carried onto the stage by the actors) and a party when the play was over. After Sophocles' time, the choregoi also had to pay for a chorus teacher or trainer.

Some men volunteered to be choregoi. They wanted the honor and glory it brought.

This monument was built in Athens in 334 BC by a wealthy choregos called Lysicrates. It was built to celebrate the success of one of his productions at the City Dionysia.

A man might object to being a choregos. When that happened, he could challenge another man to take over from him. If the other man refused to take over from him, then he had to exchange all his possessions with the challenger. This sometimes led to bitter squabbles.

The actors

Each play had three main actors, who were always men. The three actors shared all the main speaking roles between them. Even the women's parts were played by men. In the early days of Greek theatre, the poet himself was the principal actor, the protagonist. By the middle of the fifth century BC, the city of Athens provided and paid for the protagonist, allocating a paid actor to each poet.

We do not know how the other two actors were selected. Actors were paid for their performance, but they took other jobs when they were not acting.

The poet himself was responsible for telling the actors what to do. He wrote and directed the play, and until chorus trainers took over, he looked after the chorus, too.

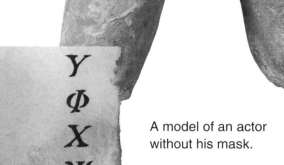

A model of an actor without his mask.

> "Dance, mother! Move those old legs this way and that . . . !"

This remark from the chorus to one of the main characters in Euripides' *Trojan Women* (415 BC) suggests that the actors and the chorus had to be quite fit.

Υ
Φ
Χ
Ψ

ΚΛΜΝΞ ΟΠΡΣΤΥΦΧΨΩ

The judges

The ten judges represented the ordinary citizens of Athens. They were not selected for their knowledge of drama. The judges were called *kritai*, from which we get the English word "critic". The kritai were chosen in a complicated way, and the punishment for trying to interfere with the process was death!

The citizens of Athens were divided into ten "tribes." Before the festival began, each tribe put

In Aristophanes' *Clouds* (423 BC), the chorus talks directly to the judges of the drama competition:

"We're keen to let the judges know
Just what they'll get if we come in first . . ."

Φ Χ Ψ

Κ Λ Μ Ν Ξ Ο Π Ρ Σ Τ Υ Φ Χ Ψ Ω

The front row of the stone seats of the theatre of Dionysus in Athens. In the center is the special throne for the priest of Dionysus.

forward the names of ten possible judges, and these names were sealed in urns (containers like jars). When the time came for the plays to be performed, the urns were opened and one name was taken from each to make up the panel of judges. The chosen ten had to swear that they would be fair when judging the plays.

The festival

A few days before the start of the festival, the program of events was announced at a ceremony known as the *proagon*. The exact order of the various parts of the festival is uncertain. But we do know that it did not begin with the drama competition.

The first festival day was a public holiday. Even prisoners were let out of jail to enjoy themselves. There was a spectacular procession, with dancing and singing and girls carrying baskets of presents. Officials wore their finest clothes, and symbols of fertility, such as flowering branches, were carried high in the air.

A maenad dancing in a procession, from the fifth century BC.

The performance begins

Before the drama competition began, the theatre was purified by sacrificing a pig. The sons of men who had been killed in war paraded before the audience. Honors were awarded to deserving citizens and foreigners, and the money paid to Athens by its allies was displayed. Finally, when the jury had been chosen, the plays began. Dithyrambs as well as plays were performed. The dithyrambs were not thought of as drama and were entered into a separate competition.

Except in times of war, there were four days of drama. The three groups of tragedies and satyr plays were performed in turn over the first three days. The last day of the festival was reserved for comedy. The order of performance was decided at the beginning of each day by drawing lots. Apparently, the last plays were thought to have the best chance of winning.

> *"Sophocles was fortunate enough to live a long time, write many fine tragedies and finally die without suffering."*
>
> Phrynichus, *Muses*, 405 BC.
>
> Ρ Σ Τ Υ Φ Χ Ψ Ω

The decision

When all the plays were over, the judges wrote the winners of their choice on pieces of pottery called potsherds. These were then placed in an urn. The archon took out five potsherds at random, and these determined the winners of the prizes for poets and producers. We do not know how the protagonists' prizes were decided. There were no prizes for the two supporting actors.

The winners were announced to the crowded theatre and then crowned with ivy, a plant sacred to Dionysus. We imagine that this ceremony was followed by victory parades and parties.

The festival was brought to an end by a special assembly in the theatre where everything that had taken place was discussed. The aim was to make sure that the festival had been properly run and to see that the next festival would be even better than the one that had just ended.

A fourth-century BC vase painting of a scene from a comedy. Watched by a slave, an old man climbs a ladder to visit his girlfriend with a present of four apples. The actors wear the padded clothing traditionally used for comic performances.

6 The Theatre

There were theatres all over ancient Greece. Some, such as the one at Epidaurus (see map on page 16), were built by one architect and have changed very little since ancient times. Most, however, have been rebuilt and altered many times over the centuries. This is what happened to the main Dionysian theatre in Athens.

No perfect example remains of a Greek theatre. Each one was different, and they changed as drama changed. In Roman times, the theatre where *Oedipus the King* was first performed was flooded in order to stage sea battles! This makes it very hard to work out precisely how it looked in Sophocles' day.

In Aristophanes' *Frogs* (405 BC), Dionysus speaks directly to the chief priest in the audience:

"You're my priest – come and help me!
I'll buy you a drink afterwards!"

Φ
Χ
Ψ

Μ Ν Ξ Ο Π Ρ Σ Τ Υ Φ Χ Ψ Ω

The seating

Greek drama was always performed in the open air. The seats rose in banks above the acting area, one row above the other, so that everyone in the audience could see what was going on.

The auditorium, where the audience sat, was usually in the shape of a semi circle. At first, the seats were made of wood. Later, the better theatres were fitted with stone benches. The front row could be 15-25 meters (50-80 feet) away from the acting area, and the back row almost 80 meters (250 feet) away. The theatre of Dionysus in Athens had eighty tiers of seats. In the front row were sixty special chairs, labeled with the names or jobs of important people, such as priests, the archon, city officials and ambassadors, who sat there. There was a special throne for the priest of Dionysus in the center of the row. Behind the priest's throne, areas were set aside for the city's council and soldiers. It was the soldiers' duty to attend the theatre to learn from the mistakes made by the characters in the plays.

The magnificent theatre in Taormina, Sicily. It was built by the Greeks in the third century BC and adapted by the Romans five centuries later. The Romans built the brickwork behind the acting area.

The audience

It is thought that the main theatre in Athens held about 17,000 spectators – more like a modern sports stadium than a theatre. The audience was made up of all sorts of people. Most were citizens of Athens, but there were also workmen, foreigners and, if they came with their masters, slaves. We do not know if women and children were allowed in.

The orchestra

The orchestra was the name given to a circular area, about 25 meters (80 feet) wide, in front of the auditorium. In the center stood an altar where sacrifices to Dionysus were made.

It is interesting to see that the the word *orchestra* – originally meaning a "dancing place" – has changed its meaning since ancient Greek times.

> An actor describes the scene in words for the audience:
> *"Imagine, carved upon these marble walls,*
> *The Gods defeating the Giants in battle."*
> Euripides, *Ion*, c. 413 BC.
>
> Φ Χ Ψ
>
> ΚΛΜΝΞΟΠΡΣΤΥΦΧΨΩ

The chorus performed on the orchestra, dancing and chanting or singing their lines. We do not know if actors went onto the orchestra when speaking with the chorus.

The acting area and skene

The acting area was on the opposite side of the orchestra from the audience. Behind it stood the *skene*. This was originally a wooden hut where the actors changed costumes and masks to play different characters.

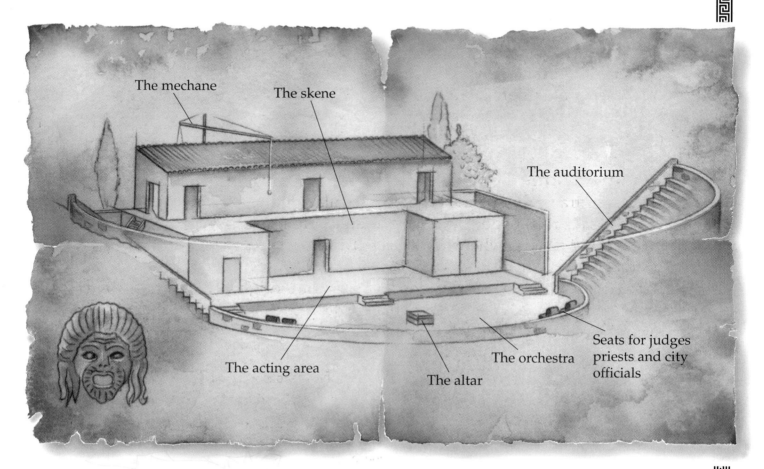

The mechane

The skene

The auditorium

The acting area

The altar

The orchestra

Seats for judges priests and city officials

In later theatres, the skene was decorated with a row of columns, known as the proscenium. The audience and chorus entered and left through doors at either side of the proscenium. The actors used doors in the skene. In time, the skene was enlarged and built of stone, giving us our words *scene* and *scenery*.

The acting area was quite a small space between the proscenium and the orchestra. It might have been slightly raised above the level of the orchestra. Actors could go higher by climbing up to the top of the proscenium. This was where the gods appeared. The larger theatres had a crane – called a *mechane* – for lifting actors to this part of the stage or for lowering them on to the stage from above.

An artist's impression of what a typical Greek theatre may have looked like. No two theatres would have been exactly the same, and we can only guess that the building behind the acting area looked like this.

7 Actors and Chorus

Actors

To the ancient Greeks, comedy acting and tragedy acting used different skills. Nevertheless, both had a number of similarities. All types of actors had to be able to sing, chant and learn their lines. They also had to be quick-witted and fit.

Above all, actors had to have magnificent voices. Modern plays have lighting, sound effects and many props to help them build an atmosphere. In Greek drama, atmosphere had to be created by voices alone.

The best protagonists were well-paid and became famous throughout the ancient Greek world. Athens sent out its protagonists as ambassadors to other states. Apart from the chorus, the two supporting actors – the *deuteragonist* and the *tritagonist* – were the other main speakers. They were not supposed to steal all the attention from the protagonist. Many plays had parts for nonspeaking extras. Apparently, Sophocles himself once came on as an extra, to the audience's delight.

As soon as they appeared, actors had to make it clear what they were doing:

"I'm on my way from the ancient oracle of Phoebus."

The character of Aegeus in Euripides' *Medea*, 431 BC.

ΥΦΧΨ

Ξ Ο Π Ρ Σ Τ Υ Φ Χ Ψ Ω

A carving of tragic and comic theatre masks from the second century AD.

Masks

Everyone on stage wore a mask. Some theatres were so huge, normal facial expressions could not be seen. The mood of a masked character could be recognized instantly. With a swift change of mask, an actor could take on another role, too.

Masks were usually made of linen, which is why they have not survived. A few were made of cork or wood. They covered the whole head and included hair, with two small eyeholes and a mouth slightly open. The mask may have acted as a megaphone, helping the actor to be heard at the back of the auditorium.

Costume and style

We know little about actors' clothing in Sophocles' time. They probably wore quite regal clothes. In comedy, they padded out their clothes to make their bodies look ridiculous.

A modern version of the sort of mask worn by a tragic actor.

A youth playing the *aulos*, sometimes translated as a flute. The aulos was the most popular musical instrument in ancient Greece. It had two pipes and a reed mouthpiece, like a modern oboe or clarinet.

Because the actors wore masks, they had to describe what the audience could not see:

"'What's the matter?
Why are you crying?
Why have you
turned so pale?"

Jason to Medea in Euripides' *Medea*, 431 BC.

Σ
Τ
Υ
Φ
Χ
Ψ

ΟΠΡΣΤΥΦΧΨΩ

The props were usually very simple – perhaps a sword was given to a warrior or a crown to a king – although sometimes objects as large as chariots appeared on stage. Because of the small size of the acting area, we assume that actors did not move around the stage as much as they do today, but it is likely that they used more gestures.

The chorus

The chorus is one of the most difficult aspects of Greek drama to understand. By the fourth century BC, even the Greeks themselves were beginning to find it odd, and it gradually went out of use. Nevertheless, in Sophocles' time, the fifteen people in the chorus were still seen as an essential part of any play. In tragedy, they normally represented a group of ordinary people, such as citizens, women or elderly men. Like the actors, members of the chorus wore masks.

In tragedy, the masks and costume of the anonymous members of the chorus were all the same. In early comedies the chorus was very important – it gave the play its name, such as *Wasps* (by Aristophanes). Comic choruses did not necessarily play people. They could be animals, or even clouds. The chorus acted as a sort of go-between, linking the actors and the audience. The chorus watched the play and also took part in it. In later comedies the chorus members only played a minor part in the play.

One of the great mysteries of Greek drama is what the chorus members did when they were not speaking. Since they filled the space between the actors and front row, they must have done something! Unfortunately, we shall never know.

The chorus in a modern performance of Aeschylus' *Oresteia* at the English National Theatre, 1981.

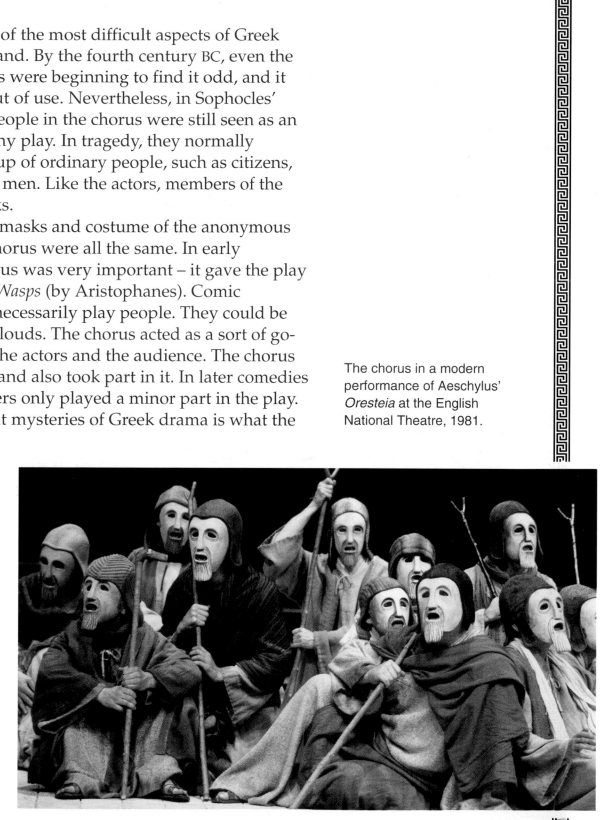

8 Playwrights

How many plays?

People who write plays are called playwrights. The ancient Greeks wrote thousands of plays. We know the titles of several hundred of them, but only forty-four complete plays have survived. We have no idea how many masterpieces have been lost.

Much of our knowledge of ancient Greek drama comes from the plays of four playwrights: Aeschylus, Sophocles, Euripides and Aristophanes. Their work represents the best plays the ancient Greeks produced. They were all written between about 484 BC, when Aeschylus first competed for the Dionysian festival prize, and 385 BC, when Aristophanes' final plays were staged.

Below is the Greek alphabet. It has twenty-four letters. How many letters can you see that we use in the English alphabet?

Above is a Roman copy of an ancient Greek portrait of the playwright Aeschylus.

$$ABΓΔEZHΘIKΛMNΞOΠPΣTYΦXΨΩ$$

Aeschylus

Aeschylus was born at Eleusis near Athens in about 525 BC. He came from a rich family, and as was expected of all Athenians, he served in the armed forces. He fought for the Athenians in their victory over the Persians at the Battle of Marathon in 490 BC.

Aeschylus wrote about seventy plays. Only seven complete ones survive, but there are fragments of others, including satyr plays. He won the City Dionysia thirteen times, the last in 458 BC. When Sophocles first beat him, in 468 BC, he was very annoyed. Aeschylus' plays are full of spectacular effects, serious dances and exciting descriptions of battles.

The three tragedies Aeschylus wrote in 458 BC (*Agamemnon*, *The Choephori* and *The Eumenides*), are known as the *Oresteia*. They make one complete story and are the only group of Greek plays to do so that survives.

Aeschylus' *Oresteia* is overshadowed by the sinister hand of Fate:

"The giant shades of Fate silently build
And pile the dim outline of the coming doom."

Agamemnon, 458 BC.

ΚΛΜΝΞΟΠΡΣΤΥΦΧΨΩ

A stone slab carved with a representation of the warrior Aristion, who fought in the great Greek victory at Marathon.

Sophocles

Like Aeschylus, Sophocles (c. 496-406 BC) was not only a writer. He served Athens, the city where he was born, in a number of ways – both in the running of the city and the army. Nevertheless, it was Sophocles' plays that brought him the greatest honor and fame. He wrote about 120 plays. Sadly, only seven of them have survived. Apparently, he won the City Dionysia eighteen times.

An actor's mask.

A carving of the first century AD (below) shows Euripides being welcomed into heaven as a god.

Many people believe that *Oedipus the King* is a very good play, so it is surprising that the group of plays of which it was a part was awarded only the second prize at the City Dionysia. The Greek philosopher Aristotle chose *Oedipus the King* as an ideal example of a tragic play.

Very few people today can understand Sophocles' original ancient Greek language, but they still admire him for the way he created exciting characters. Aristotle thought that Sophocles was responsible for introducing the third actor into Greek drama, for increasing the chorus from twelve people to fifteen, and for introducing scene painting.

Euripides

Euripides was born sometime between 485 and 480 BC. He won his first prize in the City Dionysia in 441 BC, and died in 406 BC.

Unlike the other tragic playwrights, Euripides did not play much part in the public life of Athens. He started to write after working as a painter and died abroad at the court of the king of Macedonia.

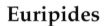

"*O God, dark ruler of the Earth, In whose eyes all things are made clear — Look down upon my crime, my sin, And see this murder foul and clear*"

The character of Orestes in Euripides' *Electra*, fifth century BC.

Ξ Ο Π Ρ Σ Τ Υ Φ Χ Ψ

Ρ Σ Τ Υ Φ Χ Ψ Ω

An actor's mask.

A tragedy mask.

Scholars do not agree about how many of Euripides' ninety-two plays survive. It is probably eighteen. One – *Rhesus* – is thought to be by another playwright. Nevertheless, more of his plays survive than of any other ancient Greek playwright. This is because Euripides' plays remained popular long after his death, and many copies of his work were made. In his own lifetime, however, he won only four or five first prizes at the City Dionysia. His *Cyclops* is the only complete satyr play to survive.

Euripides' stories are sometimes so extraordinary that in eleven of them it takes the arrival of a god to sort things out. The expression for this, "deus ex machina" (a god coming down by crane), is still used today. At the end of *Medea*, the story of a woman who murders her children, she is carried away in a chariot pulled by dragons!

Aristophanes

Aristophanes (about 445-385 BC) is the only comedy playwright whose works survive intact. We have eleven of his forty-four plays.

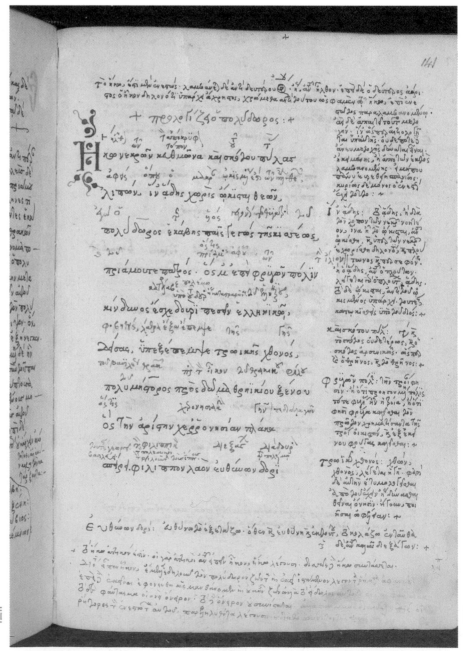

This is a copy from AD1500 of the script of Euripides' play *Hecuba*. *Hecuba* is the story of a woman who takes revenge on the king who killed her

The earliest plays by Aristophanes are sometimes known as "Old Comedy". Aristophanes' plays have remarkable plots. His characters make private peace treaties, talk with holy clouds, fly to heaven on dung beetles to complain about war, go to the underworld, or become birds. Aristophanes' plays treat gods, Athenian politicians and ordinary people with the same lack of respect. But, despite the jokes, which we can still appreciate in translations, Aristophanes' comedy always has serious things to say about Athens and its people.

In some of Aristophanes' plays the chorus dressed up as the creatures that gave their name to the play, such as *Clouds*. In one of Aristophanes' plays, *Lysistrata*, women are the heroes.

"Imagine, dear audience,
that you had wings —
You'd never need to stay
and watch the Tragic things!"
The chorus in Aristophanes' *Birds*, 414 BC.

ΚΛΜΝΞΟΠΡΣΤΥΦΧ

Υ
Φ
Χ
Ψ
Ψ Ω

A portrait of Aristophanes. Although his plays were funny, there was generally a serious message behind the humor.

9 The Legacy of Greece

Greeks and Romans

Greek theatre did not end with the death of Aristophanes. The City Dionysia continued to be held, prizes were won, and other festivals took place all over Greece. New plays were written and old ones brought back. But no other Greek playwrights left work that is finer than the Athenian playwrights of the fifth century BC.

Greece itself changed, too. During the second century BC, it came under the control of the Roman Empire. Theatres and plays were altered to suit the new rulers. The plays of the ancient Greeks were adapted for Roman audiences. Then, with the fall of the Roman Empire, the drama of ancient Greece was forgotten altogether.

Roman actors and their chorus master in rehearsal for a satyr play. The Romans took over the traditions of Greek theatre. Masks were still used, but the costumes were very different from those used in Greek drama.

The Renaissance

There were no theatres in medieval Europe, so plays were usually performed in public places. Then, at the end of the Middle Ages (about AD 1400), Europe entered a period of history known as the Renaissance (about AD 1400 to about 1600). This name means "rebirth" in French. Europeans began to take a new interest in the world of ancient Greece and Rome at this time.

Scholars looked again at the works of Greek playwrights and the places in which their works were performed. Theatres were built, some quite like the buildings used in ancient times. Greek and Roman plays influenced the work of Renaissance playwrights. Ancient Greek playwrights were once again admired and respected, and after a gap of 1,000 years, their plays were brought back to the stage. The first modern production of a translation of *Oedipus the King* took place in Italy in 1585. In some form or another, surviving ancient Greek plays have been performed regularly ever since.

The medieval view of ancient Greek life. This manuscript illustration shows Creon mourning the plague victims of Thebes. From *Oedipus the King*.

The Greek influence

Since the Renaissance, Greek drama has influenced modern theatre in five ways.

Continued performance

Greek plays have often been staged in open-air theatres, in the original Greek language using ancient Greek production methods. Many of these performances have been in Greece itself. Ancient Greek drama has also been performed all over Europe and North America.

Translations

Even more Greek plays have been performed in translation on the stage and in films. Greek works have been particularly popular in the last ten years. Recently, the English National Theatre put on the *Oresteia* with the cast wearing masks. It took them weeks of rehearsal to get used to the idea!

A nineteenth-century German painting of a Greek drama. A statue of the playwright Sophocles stands at the right of the picture. Look at the masks people are wearing on the stage.

Retelling Greek stories

From the Renaissance onwards, playwrights have retold the stories of the great Greek plays. The seventeenth-century Frenchman Jean Racine based his play *Les Plaideurs* on Aristophanes' *Wasps*. The play *Mourning Becomes Electra*, by the American playwright Eugene O'Neill (1888-1953), follows Aeschylus' *Oresteia*. O'Neill set his play in New England at the time of the American Civil War (1861-5). The modern French writer Jean Anouilh (1910-87) wrote his own versions of several Greek plays, including *Medea*. More recently, Euripides' *Bacchae* inspired *The Disorderly Woman* by John Bowen.

Ideas and inspiration

The re-discovery of ancient Greek drama has shown actors and directors fresh ways of handling plays. For example, ancient Greek theatre reminds us that huge casts and complicated sets and props are not always needed. The design of ancient Greek theatres is used in modern theatres everywhere.

Modern theatres like the Olivier Theatre in London are based on the design of ancient Greek theatres.

Part of our culture

Some of the characters and ideas in ancient Greek plays are so famous that they have become part of modern culture. The best-known example comes from *Oedipus the King*. Sigmund Freud (1856-1939) spent a lifetime trying to understand the human mind. He said that sons who were jealous of their fathers suffered from an Oedipus Complex. Freud developed this expression from Sophocles' play, written over 2,500 years earlier.

Teiresias, in a scene from the opera Oedipus Rex (Latin for Oedipus the King) by the Russian composer Igor Stravinsky. It was first performed in Paris in 1927.

". . . the Athenians employed language, action, music, painting, the dance, and religious institutions to produce the highest idealism of passion and power."

The British poet Percy Bysshe Shelly (1792-1822) in A Defence of Poetry, 1821.

Ύ Φ Χ Ψ

ΚΛΜΝΞΟΠΡΣΤΥΦΧΨΩ

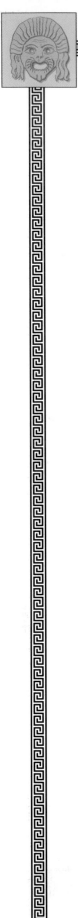

Glossary

Allies
Countries that support each other.

Ambassadors
Officials sent abroad to represent their states.

Archon
Important Athenian officials. One of the archons organized the City Dionysia.

Aristotle (384-322 BC)
A Greek philosopher who wrote books on politics, poetry, biology and anatomy.

Auditorium
A theatre's seating area.

Bacchus
Another name for Dionysus.

Choregos (plural Choregoi)
A wealthy citizen who paid for plays in a drama festival.

Chorus
The group of men who sang and danced together during a play.

Citizen
A free-born Athenian (not a slave) whose parents were Athenian.

City Dionysia
Athens' main festival in honor of Dionysus.

Deme
The name of an area of local government.

Deuteragonist
The second most important actor in an ancient Greek play.

Dithyramb
A chant, song or play in praise of the god Dionysus.

Elders
Older, respected people.

Homer
Very little is known about this poet. Legend tells us that he was blind and was born on the Greek island of Chios.

Kritai
The ten judges at the City Dionysia.

Lenaea
A festival held in Athens at the start of each February.

Macedonia
The area occupied by the kingdom of Macedon in northeast Greece.

Mechane
A crane used to lift actors on and off the stage.

Oracle
A temple or shrine where Greeks could consult the gods. People could ask the gods a question, and priests would translate noises as the words of the gods.

Orchestra
The circular area on which the chorus performed.

Proagon
The ceremony that took place a few days before the City Dionysia to announce the festival's program of events.

Prompter
Someone who stands near the stage following all the actors' speaking parts. If an actor forgets his or her lines, the prompter reminds them.

Prophecy
A prediction of the future.

Props
The shortened form of the word "properties." Properties are objects, such as swords, used by actors.

Proscenium
The building in front of the skene which eventually became an arch.

Protagonist
The most important actor.

Purify
To clean a building or area by an act of sacrifice.

Renaissance
The period of European history (c. AD 1400 to c. 1600) when a new interest was shown in classical culture.

Rural Dionysia
Dionysian festivals in demes and villages.

Sacred
An object, place or person closely connected to a religion.

Sacrifice
Killing an animal to please a god.

Scholar
Someone who is an expert in one or more areas of knowledge.

Seer
Someone who predicts the future.

Skene
The backdrop to the stage.

Thespis
A poet of the sixth century BC who is supposed to have been the first man to act separately from the chorus.

Tiers
Rows of seats, each set back from and above the one before.

Tragedy
A serious, sad play.

Translation
Changing written or spoken words into different languages.

Tribute money
Money paid by one state to a more powerful one.

Tritagonist
The third most important actor in a Greek play.

Time Line

BC

750-700 Greek alphabet comes into use. Homer composing the *Iliad* and the *Odyssey*.

580 Temple built to Athena in Athens.

534 First tragedy performed at City Dionysia.

c. 525 Aeschylus born.

501 First satyr play performed at City Dionysia.

c. 496 Sophocles born.

490 Battle of Marathon: Greeks defeat Persian invaders.

486 First comedy performed at City Dionysia.

c. 485 Euripides born.

484 First victory of Aeschylus at City Dionysia.

468 Sophocles first defeats Aeschylus in City Dionysia. Three actors used in plays.

458 Aeschylus' *Oresteia.*

456 Death of Aeschylus.

455 First production of a play by Euripides.

c. 445 Aristophanes born.

c. 440 Drama competition in Lenaea festival.

431 Euripides' *Medea.*

422 Aristophanes' *Wasps.*

415 Euripides' *Trojan Women.*

411 Aristophanes' *Lysistrata.*

c. 406/5 Sophocles and Euripides die.

393-385 Last plays of Aristophanes.

c. 385 Aristophanes dies.

Further Information

Books to read
Ancient Greece. John D. Clare. Harcourt Brace, 1994.
Ancient Greece. Roger Lancelyn Green. The John Day Co., 1977.
What Life Was Like at the Dawn of Democracy: Classical Athens, 525-322BC. Time-Life Books, 1997.

Books for older readers
Greek Tragedy in Action. Oliver Taplin. Routledge, 1994.
Images of the Greek Theatre. Richard Green & Eric Handley. University of Texas Press, 1995.
Greek Tragedy. Humphrey D. Kitto. Routledge Chapman & Hall, 1961.

The Greek plays in translation
The Complete Greek Tragedies, 4 vols. David Grene & Richmond Lattimore, eds. University of Chicago Press, 1992.
Seven Famous Greek Plays. Whitney Oates & Eugene O'Neill, Jr., eds. Random House, 1996.

Good paperback editions exist in Penguin Classics, Bantam Classics, and Signet Classics.

Places to visit
If you are ever lucky enough to spend a vacation in Greece or go there on a school trip, you will be able to see original Greek theatres. The most complete example is at Epidaurus.

Photographic acknowledgments
The publishers would like to thank the following sources for providing photographs:
AKG, London 4, 11, 44; **Ancient Art & Architecture/Ronald Sheridan** cover, 3, 5, 13 (bottom), 15, 19, 25, 32, 33, 37, 41, 42; **Bridgeman Art Library** 7 (also detail), 43; **British Library**, London 40; **Donald Cooper/Photostage** 35; **Donald Cooper/ Photostage/English National Opera** 45 (bottom); **C.M. Dixon** 6, 8, 13 (top), 28-9, 36, 38-9; **e.t. archive** 18, 20; **Sonia Halliday** 21; **Michael Holford** 9, 12, 14, 22, 23, 24, 27, 34; **National Theatre**, London 45 (top); **University of Bristol Theatre Collection** 10; **Werner Forman Archive** 17.   **Maps and illustration:** HardLines

Index

Numbers in **bold** indicate an illustration.
Words in **bold** can be found in the glossary on page 46.